DISCUSSION PAPER 54

Reflections on the Challenge of Reconstructing Post-Conflict States in West Africa
INSIGHTS FROM CLAUDE AKE'S POLITICAL WRITINGS

JEREMIAH O. AROWOSEGBE

NORDISKA AFRIKAINSTITUTET, UPPSALA 2011

Indexing terms
Political development
Democratization
Post-conflict reconstruction
State
Nation-building
Peacebuilding
Political theory
Nigeria, Niger Delta
Sierra Leone

Language checking: Peter Colenbrander
ISSN 1104-8417
ISBN 978-91-7106-689-3
© the author and Nordiska Afrikainstitutet 2011
Grafisk Form Elin Olsson, ELBA Grafisk Produktion
Print on demand, Lightning Source UK Ltd.

Contents

Foreword

This Discussion Paper is based on the theoretical exploration of the challenges of state-reconstruction in West Africa, drawing on the postulations of Nigeria's foremost political scientist and theorist, Claude Ake, who died in a plane crash in 1996. It is based on a critique of 'externally driven post-conflict state-reconstruction projects' in the sub-region, drawing extensively on the cases of Sierra Leone, which experienced brutal civil wars in the 1990s, and Nigeria's oil-rich Niger Delta region, which has been immersed in insurgent violence since 2006. Rather than state-reconstruction, the author argues in favour of state-transformation, based on Ake's call for 'endogenous initiatives of rebuilding the state from below' as a fundamental step towards sustainable democratic peacebuilding in West Africa.

The paper's point of departure is the refutation of the view that the state project in Africa is 'hopeless' or at a dead-end. While acknowledging the shortcomings of the state-formation project in some countries, the author takes the view that the state on the continent remains a key institutional and social actor, which needs to be understood more in terms of its historical moorings, political economy and (subordinate) place in the international system. The paper also establishes a case for interrogating hegemonic discourses on the nature of the state in Africa and post-conflict peacebuilding on the continent.

Drawing on Ake's notion of the limited autonomy of the state in Africa, which renders it susceptible to capture by hegemonic elites and thus to becoming a site for intra-elite struggles for power, as well as an actor in conflict against excluded and marginalised social groups, the author holds that the nature of the state in West Africa renders it prone to violent conflict. In this regard, the connections between the predatory character of the state and the descent into violent conflict in Sierra Leone are critically analysed. This is followed by an analysis of the decline of the authority of the Nigerian state in the Niger Delta, and the open challenge to its legitimacy by a coterie of insurgent militias.

Following the two West African case studies, the paper interrogates the epistemological groundings of mainstream peacebuilding discourses, and argues there is no guarantee that models imported on the basis of such postulates would ensure sustainable peace in Africa. On this basis, a compelling case is made for reinventing the state in Africa, based on autochthonous democratic transformation in favour of the ordinary people. The original contribution made by this paper can be found in its arguments for an endogenous transformation of the state in ways that can strongly root it in its people and their popular aspirations and as a fundamental step towards sustainable peace and breaking the vicious cycle of crisis on the continent. This paper will be interest to political theorists, scholars on peace and conflict in Africa and those interested in the relevance of the works of contemporary African thinkers to the development challenges facing the continent.

Cyril Obi
Senior Researcher
The Nordic Africa Institute

Abstract

This paper[1] addresses a theoretical gap on state-transformation as a step towards sustainable peace, and discusses the relevance of Ake's political thought for state-reconstruction in post-conflict West Africa. It underscores the need for the autochthonous transformation of the state as a central component of peacebuilding and post-conflict transition on the continent, as Ake had suggested. Drawing on illustrations from two West African cases – Sierra Leone and Nigeria's oil-rich Niger Delta – it explores Ake's works on 'the state in Africa' against the backdrop of 'externally driven state-reconstruction projects' hinged on global hegemonic discourses on nation-building in post-conflict situations. The paper also reviews Ake's thought as a basis for critiquing ongoing state rehabilitation attempts and urges a return to 'endogenous initiatives of rebuilding the state from below' as a condition for achieving a 'sustainable democratic reconstruction of the state' in post-conflict Africa. Arguing that state-building in Africa was neither tragedy nor farce, this paper, in the context of Ake's critique of the colonial discourse on the state in Africa, makes a case for a more sustainable alternative based on endogenous initiatives for rebuilding the post-conflict state in West Africa from below.

Keywords: Claude Ake, Nigeria's Niger Delta region, Sierra Leone, state reconstruction, post-conflict West Africa.

---

1. This is part of a wider study (PhD thesis) on the political thought of Claude Ake.

Introduction

The state in Africa has had a chequered history. Its trajectory is therefore best understood by contextualising its myriad challenges under changing historical experiences. In the immediate post-independence period, the crucial problem was the integration of the 'new state,' which was threatened by strong centrifugal forces (Ake 1967a:17). 'Nation-building' and 'political integration' thus emerged as important themes in the theoretical thinking on Africa in the literature of that era (Coleman 1955; Wriggins 1961; Ake 1967b, 1973 and 1974; Lijphart 1971; Syed 1980). The 1950s and 1960s witnessed the ascendancy of the state in both theoretical and policy considerations of the African predicament, with several efforts made to strengthen relevant institutions as a way out of the legacy of underdevelopment and dependency (Agbaje 1991:723).

This study discusses the relevance of Ake's political thought to state-reconstruction in post-conflict West Africa. It provides an insight into his works and his contribution to the problematic of this study. Focusing on Sierra Leone and Nigeria's Niger Delta, it highlights the background to the complex web of violent conflicts and wars that ravaged the sub-region in the 1990s and the ways in which the newly won peace poses challenges to the reconstruction of post-conflict states in the sub-region. The aim is to advance an autochthonous perspective on the conditions for reinventing the state in Africa for the purpose of promoting democracy, reconciliation and development.

This study is framed against the backdrop of the rather destructive civil wars that many African states have passed through. Within such polities, the imperative of the postwar reconstruction of damaged economies, devastated and divided societies and the entire process of healing old wounds continue to be writ large. Hence, there is a need for detailed studies of post-conflict transitions on the continent with a view to arriving at viable options for reconstructing state and society in ways that enhance inclusive and sustainable peace, security and development. These experiences of ecological stresses, widespread socioeconomic problems, identity politics, unrest as well as the pressures for democratisation underline the need to examine the ongoing dynamics of conflict and peacebuilding across the continent, in addition to interrogating the roles played by local, national, regional and international actors in negotiating post-conflict transitions to post-war reconstruction.

This paper posits that, in spite of its failings, the state in Africa cannot be written off as an entirely hopeless case. Notwithstanding the obeisance of neoliberals to globalisation and its imperatives, the state in Africa is still a major conceptual and institutional actor, especially on the international stage (Dossa 1998).

Which factors undermine state cohesion in post-conflict West Africa? How can such inhibitions be overcome? And how relevant is Ake's political thought to state reconstruction in the sub-region? This paper answers these questions. As is widely known, Africa is a deeply contested ideological and intellectual terrain (Zeleza 1997:iii). This is especially the case within the debates on globalisation (Slater 1998). In this connection, the extent to which Africa's 'colonial past' still influences its 'postcolonial present' is a subject of continuing debate.

The case for exploring Ake's writing as a basis for critiquing hegemonic discourses on post-conflict peacebuilding in West Africa needs to be well established. The point of departure in this study of Ake's political thought is that it is both relevant to, and important in a process of rethinking the African state and its crises and exploring the options for its reconstruction. This is against the background of many scholarly works on political theorists in Africa focusing on their contributions to the colonial liberation struggles in various countries, or in some cases, cynically casting aspersions on the relevance of contemporary African political thought.

Ake's postulations on the state in Africa have attracted numerous responses from both the African and Africanist literature. The role of elections, decentralisation and federalism in post-conflict state-reconstruction are areas where Ake's thoughts have challenged neoliberal orthodoxy, but also where they have come under challenge. Ake's analyses of these issues have also been critiqued by scholars in other works (Mafeje 1997 and Efemini 2000). Brilliantly argued and carefully situated within an uncompromising neo-Marxist perspective, Ake's theoretical construction of the state in Africa is broad and covers a complex range of issues, including the historiography of the state; the nature and character of the state; the relationship between state and social classes; the state, development and underdevelopment; the state and democratisation; the state and the national question; the operation and internal mechanisms of a dependent capitalist state as well as the unique features of the state in Africa. Locating itself within this wide array of issues, this paper connects Ake's thesis on 'the limited autonomy' of the state in Africa to the propensity for conflicts and civil wars in West Africa. The critique of Ake's thoughts; the making of his life, career and scholarship; as well as other developments and issues which influenced different periods and aspects of his thought have been treated in greater detail elsewhere (Arowosegbe 2008). Rather, it is the relevance of his critique of mainstream Western social science, particularly the critique of Africa's political economy, elite politics and the impact of the adoption of neoliberal policies to address the crisis of development facing the continent that stands out in sharp relief when applied to post-conflict contexts.

This paper is divided into seven sections. The first presents a background to Ake's thinking on the state in Africa and its relevance to state-reconstruction in post-conflict settings. The second discusses state collapse and subversion in West Africa from the immediate post-Cold War period. Section three examines the political crisis that crippled Sierra Leone's democratic stability in the 1990s. Section four discusses state decline and other weaknesses characterising the Nigerian state through the exiting of the state by its citizens and the development of anti-state mobilisations, almost on the scale of an insurgency. Section five critiques the hegemonic discourse on peacebuilding and state-reconstruction in post-conflict West Africa. Claude Ake's contribution to reinventing the state in Africa, especially in post-conflict societies is explored section six, while section seven provides the conclusion.

Claude Ake's thoughts on the state in Africa

How does Ake conceptualise the state in Africa? What are the implications of his thoughts on the state for understanding political thought on the continent? How does he relate the character of the state to conflict in Africa? This section provides some answers. It underlines the central elements of Ake's thesis on the state in Africa. Statehood not only represents a body of institutions, but also a set of attitudes that we associate with civilisation. It is also an everyday reality, which we cannot afford to ignore (Jalee 1977). Issues impinging on the state are therefore deeply contentious, not just for political theorists but also for members of the dominant classes of every society, particularly capitalist societies (Poulantzas 1978). Nothing has been more central to social and political theory than the issues concerning the nature and powers of the state. David Held (1985:1-6) describes them as 'real issues' and 'great matters of politics' in relation to which unlimited conflicts of interest and interpretation are bound to exist.

Ake (1985a:105) defines the state as a set of relationships and interactions among social classes and groups organised and sustained by political power:

> The state is a specific modality of class domination. This modality is one in which class domination is mediated by commodity exchange so that the system of institutional mechanisms of domination is differentiated and dissociated from the ruling class and even the society, and appears as an objective force standing alongside society. The essential feature of the state form of domination is that the system of institutional mechanisms of domination is autonomized and becomes largely independent of the social classes, including the hegemonic class.

Although he acknowledges the existence of other 'non-capitalist' forms of state domination, he presents the state as essentially a capitalist phenomenon and locates the particularities of the capitalist mode of production as the ideal typical setting for the development of the state form of domination.

According to Ake (1985a:106), the thorough-going generalisation of commodity production and exchange, which characterises this mode of production, allows for the high degree of autonomisation of class domination. He demonstrates this by illustrating 'the relationship between the pervasive autonomisation of commodity exchange' and 'the autonomisation of class domination.' He stresses that under the capitalist mode of production, particularly under conditions of 'pervasive commoditisation,' which include that of labour power, society becomes highly 'atomised' such that people are first and foremost commodity bearers, even when their sole commodity is their labour power. In the process, society is reduced increasingly and perpetually to a market economy, operated and governed by the logic of the market and the dictates of capital, and social life revolves around the norms of individualism and competition, such that as they pursue their particular interests, members of this market economy become individually interdependent and collectively dependent on the forces of the market. Such forces of the market are reproduced through their daily interactive decisions, which appear as an independent force that subordinates and dominates them. Ake (1985a:106) calls this 'the autonomizing matrix of domination for solidarity,' which coerces all into interdependence and subordination, and behind which is the domination of man by man and the domination of labour by capital. These, according to him, are constituted in such a manner that economic domination seems to operate independently of the social groups that dominate and is therefore perceived as a natural force within society, or at any rate, as an impersonal market force.

He captures 'autonomisation' as 'the very essence of the state' and identifies 'the autonomisation of the mechanisms of domination' as the central feature of the state both in political theory and also in advanced capitalist societies (Ake 1985a:106-7). According to him, this does not mean that the state is entirely neutral, but that it is significantly autonomous and independent of the existing social and hegemonic classes within it. In his view, the state's autonomisation is concretely expressed in two ways. In this regard, he noted that 'autonomisation … institutionalizes the equal treatment of unequals that underlies the capital relation' (sic) (1985a:107). He goes on further to note: 'Thus epitomized as the rule of law, autonomisation reproduces the rule of capital over labor by the very rights it guarantees, for example, the worker's right to sell his labor to whoever he or she pleases, the capitalist's right to surplus value and its free disposal.'

Ake argues that with regard to Africa, an understanding of the history, nature and character of the state is very important to capturing the dynamics of socioeconomic formations, their configuration and transformation within it. This, according to Ake (1985b:1-32), is because the state is the central locus of politics and therefore the major determinant of the direction of most societal processes. He traces the history of the state in Africa to (i) colonialism and the capitalist penetration of the region (Ake 1981:19-31 and 32-42) and (ii) the eventual political legacy of colonialism for the continent (Ake 1996a:1-6). Having characterised the capitalist mode of production as 'the ideal setting' for the development of the state form of domination, Ake refrains from referring to the social formations in Africa as 'independent states.' This, according to him, is because the specific form of capitalist development that occurred in Africa is both 'enclave and peripheral.' Furthermore, he notes that 'the process of state formation on the continent is bogged down by knotty contradictions, which stubbornly resist transcendence' (Ake 1985b:3). Speaking to these contradictions, he refers to the wholesale importation of the mentalities, practices and routines of the colonial state into its postcolonial successor and the limited nature of the state's independence that results from that process (Ake 1996a:1-6). According to him, 'In Africa, there are few social formations that are capitalist enough or socialist enough to be identifiable as clearly boasting the state form of domination' (Ake 1985a:108).

Ake argues that far from being overwritten, significant legacies of Africa's 'colonial past' still influence the 'postcolonial state' in remarkable ways (Ake 1996a). He identifies 'limited autonomy' as 'the unique feature of the state in Africa' (Ake 1985a:108-10) and points out that that the limited autonomy of the postcolonial state furthers its dependent and peripheralised status within the polarised system of global capitalism. In doing this, he draws attention to the role of the state, which he describes as central to the worldwide polarisation of the capitalist system by intensifying dependence on the metropolitan economies. Politically, he observes that in spite of independence, the absoluteness, arbitrariness and statism of the colonial state crept in intact into its postcolonial heir and still defines its character as an autocratic and exclusive state, which alienates the people in economic and political decision-making processes (Ake 1996a:1-3). Economically, he maintains that the dependence, disarticulation and other contradictions of the colonial economy still loom large (Ake 1981:44-65). According to Ake (2000:115-16):

> For the most part, at independence the colonial state was inherited by the indigenous elite rather than being liquidated or transformed. As was the case with the colonial state, the distinguishing characteristic of the post-colonial state in Africa is its lack of autonomy; power was highly fused and used by those in control of the state simply as the instrument for serving their own interests.

He dismisses the notion of failed development in Africa and argues that development has never really been on the continent's agenda in the first place. He captures 'political conditions,' defined in terms of 'the struggle for power,' 'political survival' and 'other exigencies of the elites' as the greatest impediment to development on the continent and identifies 'the poverty of ideas' as remarkable in this regard (Ake 1996a:1 and 19). To him, this explains the foisting of the development burden on other countries and the adoption of 'dependent development' as a strategy for socioeconomic transformation by the elites. Quoting extensively, Ake (1996a:19) remarks that:

> In the final analysis, dependent development was a politically driven decision hinging on considerations of political survival, considerations that impelled African leaders to marginalize development and even their role in its pursuit. It is indicative of their limited commitment to development that with few exceptions, African countries came to independence with hardly any discernible vision of development and no agenda for its realisation. Most of the newly independent countries relied heavily on expatriates for their development plans, which were usually collections of policy targets and programs that took for granted the validity of the inherited economic structure.

The limited autonomy of the state in Africa engenders conflict in a number of ways (Ake 1997:1-5). This is because the stakes in the struggles for state power are very high and factional competition often assumes 'a zero-sum game approach.' In the process, the state is ensnared in the struggles by contending elements and is often hijacked by the hegemonic social classes within it. According to Ake, this leads to an exclusive politics articulated in the struggle for power based on efficiency norms rather than legitimacy norms; the triumph of the vicious over the virtuous circle; centralisation of power; imposition of domination and political control; alienation of leaders from their masses; and the deployment of extremism in the exercise of power. In effect, the 'people tendentially retreat into primary groups which become the beneficiary of their residual loyalty' (Ake 1996a:3) and explore other 'extra-juridical' and 'non-state means,' which often have very high conflict potential. In the process, society becomes deeply divided and alienation is endemic, while distrust and anxiety among the contending groups are so pronounced that the state stumbles and totters on the brink of disaster, almost headed for disintegration in a cycle of political violence, recrimination and war (Ake 1982:1-3).

Under these circumstances, state-building is subverted and becomes the political equivalent of primitive accumulation 'in a rather violent form' (Ake 1997:2). It entails conquest and subjugation, since it is projected as arbitrary power. It revokes the autonomy of communities and subjects them to 'alien rule' within an otherwise independent political system (i) by laying claim to the resources of subordinated territories and (ii) through its exertion of 'legitimate force' in counteracting resource wars and pro-democratic resistance (Ake 1997:2). State-building in Africa thus assumes a rather violent character as groups or social classes jostle for power and resources.

State collapse and subversion in West Africa

The theoretical status of the state in Africa has received much attention in the literature and should not detain us here. While state failure refers to the 'functional' erosion of the 'state's capacity' in relation to the functions that modern states should fulfil, state collapse refers to the 'disintegration' of 'state authority.' Full-blown state collapse thus entails the 'total disintegration' of 'public authority' and the descent of societies into a battlefield of all against all, a rather rare occurrence across the world (Milliken and Krause 2002:753). While Nigeria may be categorised as 'a weak state' in which the state has been unable to maintain security and public order, provide 'legitimate representation' as well as wealth and welfare to the citizens in the oil-rich Niger Delta region, state collapse has occurred at different periods in Liberia, Somalia and the Democratic Republic of Congo. The descriptive phrase 'complex political emergencies' therefore illustrates the present context of 'state crisis' in Africa (Allen 1999:367). Both cases contain (i) an indicative understanding of the 'stateness' against which the state under examination is measured as having succeeded or failed – the 'institutional' dimension of state collapse; and (ii) the normative and practical implications of such a failure – the 'functional' dimension of state failure (Milliken and Krause 2002:753-5).

This paper examines the intra-state conflicts and political instability in West Africa as consequences of the limited autonomy of the state in Africa. Conflicts and wars on the continent have also been ascribed to other causes and factors, including 'reduction in a country's per capita GDP,' 'narrowing of the political space and institutions,' 'the role of material incentives in motivating rebellions,' 'the relationship between rebel leaders and followers' as well as 'the absence of democratic reforms to manage the challenges associated with the diversity of African societies.' In addition to their limited autonomy, which limits the capacity of the state to mediate among competing demands and conflicts, the state itself becomes both an actor in and a site of conflict. Thus, the political crisis in Sierra Leone and Nigeria's Niger Delta are connected to both the limited autonomy of the state in both countries and to a related governance failure that incorporated them into a conflict system, namely the predatory nature of the states and the rent-seeking dispositions of their ruling elites.

State collapse in Sierra Leone

Although Sierra Leone was a promising constitutional democracy during the first six years after decolonisation (1961-67), its recent war experience represents one of the most tragic episodes in the country's post-independence history (Cheru 2008:5). Its political crisis began shortly after Sir Milton Margai, the country's first prime minister and leader of the Sierra Leone People's Party (SLPP), died in office in 1964 and was replaced as party leader and prime minister by his half-brother, Albert Margai (Kandeh 2003:191). Albert Margai's leadership of the SLPP triggered dissension within the party and led to the defection of prominent northern leaders, who later joined the opposition, the All People's Congress (APC). When the APC defeated the SLPP in the second post-independence elections of 1967, Albert Margai and other SLPP stalwarts encouraged the army commander at the time to seize power. This intervention seriously undermined a smooth transfer of power. It also marked a major reversal in the country's emerging democratic system. Although the APC was eventually installed a year later, the country's progress towards democratic governance had already been derailed.

The APC was in power in Sierra Leone between 1968 and 1992. These years were marred by corruption and repression among state officials (Kandeh 2003:192). The four general elections (1973, 1977, 1982, 1987) conducted under the APC were fraudulent. In addition to political repression and leadership corruption, the economy slipped into a deep crisis. There was de-industrialisation, corruption and dependence on the petty-commodity sector for social reproduction (Bangura 1992). Economic devastation was particularly evident in the extractive sector (Kandeh 1996:401). These situations engendered alienation and 'sowed the seeds of armed rebellion and subaltern terror' in the country (Kandeh 2003:192). In March 1991, the Revolutionary United Front (RUF) led by Foday Sankoh, and supported by Charles Taylor's National Patriotic Front fore Liberia invaded entered Sierra Leone from its eastern borders. It appeared at the time that Foday, an ex-corporal in the Sierra Leonean Army was intent on overthrowing the government of Joseph Momoh which he accused of corruption and misrule. The RUF quickly established a foothold in the eastern part of the country plunging the country into civil war. In 1992, the situation was compounded when members of the military underclass in the country's army – 'the militariat' – captured state power in a successful coup against the Momoh administration and reconstituted the government under a military junta, the National Provisional Ruling Council (NPRC). As Kandeh (2003:192) observes: 'The RUF rebellion hastened the removal of the APC in a *coup d'état* orchestrated by junior officers of the Sierra Leone army. The APC's ouster in a popular coup rekindled public expectations for an end to the RUF rebellion, the restoration of state capacities and a return to democratic rule.'

However, contrary to its populist rhetoric, the NPRC failed to adopt socially transformative goals. It also failed to create new mobilising political structures. It was, in fact, not fundamentally different from its predecessor, especially because it could neither end the civil war nor restore the state. It should be noted that in Sierra Leone signs of institutional collapse predated the NPRC. Such signs were among the reasons given for ousting the APC. Nevertheless, the emergence of the militariat as a major contender for power in the country highlights some of the pitfalls of clientelism as a mechanism of political domination (Kandeh 1996:388). The subaltern militariat was mainly a disruptive political force, which accelerated state collapse through the dual usurpation of military command and political leadership. In understanding its emergence, attention should be paid to elite practices in the country, which created the conditions that allowed subalterns to usurp power and terrorise society (Kandeh 1999:349-66). These conditions came about through the appropriation of lumpen violence and thuggery by the political class, a process that undermined security and paved the way for the emergence of armed marginalised youths whose activities crippled and undermined governance in a remarkable way.

Eventually, the NPRC became a major source of instability in the Sierra Leonean state. This was evident in the state's descent into predation and the use of violence, a development that heralded the dawn of 'a new barbarism'. These activities further weakened the state and led to the fragmentation of power and the breakdown of law and order, signalling the collapse of the state as protective and regulatory institution in the final years of military rule. The corollary was the reduction of the state's extractive and allocative capacities, especially as capital flight created a domestic liquidity crisis (Kandeh 1996:400-1). On balance, the collapse of the state in Sierra Leone created problems for democratisation, state capacity and institution-building (Kandeh 1996:397-404). Growing public demands and external pressures for multiparty elections later compelled the NPRC to conduct elections and hand over power in 1996. Several issues have characterised the country's return to democratic politics.

Although the country has recovered from its former failed status, with elections held in 1996, 2002 and 2007, the actual costs of democratic transitions (Zack-Williams 2008), state collapse (Callaghy 1994) and the challenges of peacebuilding in the context of post-conflict reconstruction of the state still loom large (Ottaway 2003). Several threats have also confronted the state in Sierra Leone and attracted the attention of regional and international actors. Some of these issues have engaged other scholars, but this study's focus is on the limitations of ongoing state reconstruction initiatives and the prospects for rebuilding democracies and virile economies in the aftermath of violent conflict. Thus, rather than undertaking a detailed analysis of the conflict in Sierra Leone and Nigeria's oil-rich Niger Delta, this study focuses primarily on the critique of hegemonic discourses on state reconstruction in West Africa using Ake's postulations on the political economy of Africa.

State decline in Nigeria's oil-producing Niger Delta

Although total state collapse has not occurred in Nigeria during its postcolonial history, the Niger Delta illustrates the case of a frontal challenge to the legitimacy of the state by local insurgent groups. These groups attack the symbols of the state and oil companies for their roles in the wanton exploitation and pollution of the oil-rich region, roles they also see as the outcome of the marginalisation and impoverishment of the ethnic minorities that produce the oil that fuels the federal government of Nigeria. Thus, the Niger Delta struggle is anchored on agitations for 'resource control,' 'true federalism,' 'self-determination' and an end to decades of 'internal colonialism' by multinational capital and the majority ethnic groups through the operation of a skewed federal structure (Harneit-Sievers 2006; Uche 2008).

The Niger Delta question is embedded in a historical quest for self-determination and justice in the sharing of the oil-wealth. However, there is also the factor of inter-elite struggles over oil revenues. Given the rather predatory and rentier character of the Nigerian state, especially in the context of an oil-centric political economy and the legacies of military rule, the high stakes in controlling oil have often led to sacrificing the citizenship rights of the ethnic minorities of the oil-producing region. The violent conflict in the region has had serious implications for the country's stability and security. The politics of oil-revenue allocation in Nigeria have engendered violent conflict through the competition for oil revenues by ethnically defined constituencies (Williams 1980:69), as have 'the politics of neglect and repression' adopted by successive regimes in response to agitations for redress by people the region (Cooper 2006:174). On the impact on Nigeria's cohesion and stability of the violent uprising in the region, Ake (1996b:34) observes that 'what is at issue is nothing less than the viability of Nigeria, as oil is the real power and the stuff of politics in Nigeria as well as what holds the country in a fragile dialectical unity of self-seeking. It is time to call Shell to order and to account.'

The agitation by the Movement for the Survival of the Ogoni People (MOSOP) in the early 1990s was limited to the Ogoni, but currently there is an explosion of violent conflict on the scale of an insurgency that has been fatal across the region and with telling effects on national development. Taking the form of 'attacks against oil firms and Nigerian military personnel protecting oil complexes and installations' (Ukiwo 2007:587) as well as 'hostage taking and hijackings' (Suberu 2004:338), the Niger Delta crisis is presently the greatest challenge to Nigerian federalism as an instrument for managing ethnic-territorial cleavages and fiscal challenges (David-West 1994:33; Ejobowah 2000:29-47).

Nigeria's return to civilian rule in May 1999 raised expectations of political change in the country. When these expectations were not quickly met, political pressures and tensions were exacerbated in the country. Examples of these were inter-governmental conflicts, constitutional and institutional crises as well as ethno-regional and religious tensions in different parts of the country. With regard to the Niger Delta crisis, the response of the Nigerian state has been mixed, a carrot and stick policy that most local people consider insufficient to meet their genuine aspirations and rights. Such responses have also created a situation in which the capacity for violence by previously marginalised armed groups and young combatants has become a new marker of elitism and a source of leverage on peace agreements (Ismail 2008:259-78). Examples of similar responses abound in the country's colonial and postcolonial histories.

In the early 1990s, rather than respond to MOSOP's demands (Suberu 2008), the then military government crushed Ogoni resistance by unleashing the military on the community and through the trial and hanging of Ken Saro-Wiwa and eight other MOSOP activists in November 1995 (Obi 2006:96-8). However, the military repression of the Ogoni failed to stem the tide of protest and violence in the region as other communities confronted oil companies and one another in bitter conflict. In December 1998, the Ijaw Youth Council (IYC) issued the Kaiama Declaration in which it claimed ownership of the oil in Ijawland and asked all oil company contractors and personnel to withdraw from Ijawland by 30 December 1998 pending resolution of the question of 'resource ownership' and control of the Ijaw area of the delta (The Kaiama Declaration 1998). In response, the federal government declared a state of emergency in the region and deployed thousands of soldiers, naval troops and anti-riot policemen to protect oil installations and investments, while also dispersing Ijaw protesters. During the violent exchanges that ensued, some protesters and others suspected of being IYC members or supporters were arrested, with a handful of individuals killed (Obi 2006).

In May 1999, Chevron Texaco allegedly transported Nigerian military personnel in its helicopters, from which they shot and killed two protesters on Chevron Texaco's Parabe oil platform (Obi 2006). Later that year, in November, federal troops razed the oil-producing town of Odi for failing to produce a criminal gang suspected of murdering seven policemen. In the process, about 2,000 inhabitants of Odi lost their lives while others were displaced (Ukiwo 2007). As Obi (2006:96) observes, 'the operation at Odi fitted a regular pattern in which the Nigerian state deployed maximum force to deter and contain threats to oil interests and oil companies in the region.' Far from ending conflict, such responses have further militarised the region, with violent conflict escalating along communal lines.

Although the ineffectiveness of the Nigerian state in resolving the Niger Delta crisis is real, the underlying factors have yet to be fully explored. There are deeper structural problems associated with the character of Nigerian elites and the neocolonial character of the Nigerian economy (Ake 1996). Consideration of these failings enhances understanding of the problems impinging on the social transformation of the Nigerian state and its economy. The state's responses to violent conflict in the region reflect the economic interests of its ruling class, which seeks to uphold the conditions for uninterrupted oil production. In accordance with its objective situation, this class conceptualises state control of the resources of subordinated territories as 'national interest,' to be safeguarded through the exertion of 'legitimate force' to repress the demands for the equitable redistribution of oil revenues in favour of the people of the Niger Delta.

These failings are implicit in the oil-dependent nature of the state and the limited commitment of its ruling elite to economic and social transformation. The state's repressive disposition reflects the consciousness of the Nigerian dominant elite, which uses its capture of the oil-state apparatus to advance its narrow class and personal interests. In effect, the elite's operations do not prioritise national interest. Its politics are largely defined by strategies to ensure its dominance and prosperity as a ruling elite, including protecting the economic, strategic and energy interests of its partners, the multinational oil corporations. The Nigerian elite is also keen to increase its share of surplus from oil revenue in relation to metropolitan capital (Ake 1985b:195-200). This disposition underlines the state's tendency to monopolise oil revenues and the country's continuing external economic dependence as well as internal political instability (Graf 1988).

The objective character of the Nigerian ruling elite renders the Niger Delta crisis intractable. The elite insists on controlling federal power as a means (i) to intervene in the economic process, (ii) to create the material basis for its domination and (iii) to maintain the political conditions for accumulation. As Andre Gunder Frank (1981:188) puts it, under these circumstances, far from being neutral, the state becomes the principal instrument in the hands of local and metropolitan elites to intensify the conditions necessary for perpetuating 'super-exploitation':

The state is the principal instrument used by capital to create, maintain, extend and intensify the political conditions necessary for superexploitation, particularly... around the Third World. The state functions as the watchdog of super-exploitation by repressing first and foremost labor and its organisations, and then by imposing 'austerity' measures on the general population through 'emergency' rule, constitutional 'reform,' and martial 'law.' These austerity measures are oftentimes enforced through repressive military regimes and then institutionalized through military and civilian authoritarian states.

The experiences in Sierra Leone and Nigeria's Niger Delta confirm Ake's position on the implications of the limited autonomy of the state in Africa. The underlying thesis that emerges from the foregoing analysis is that conservative elite politics, by their very tendency to mobilise and prioritise on the political agenda the control and sharing of state power and resources, exacerbate conflicts and tensions, and therefore make their management a critical matter not just for the success of democratisation, but also for the survival of the state (Osaghae 1994:31). The rather unstable nature of elite politics and state dependency on oil explain the vulnerability of the Nigerian state to violent conflict, not least over oil and other natural resources. In the next section, we critique ongoing state-building projects in order to lay bare the ways in which they either undermine or strengthen the state's capacity for peacebuilding and post-conflict reconstruction in Sierra Leone and the Niger Delta.

State reconstruction in post-conflict West Africa

How relevant are hegemonic discourses on peacebuilding and post-conflict reconstruction in West Africa? And what lessons do our case studies suggest in terms of institution-building and state capacity? This section answers these questions. Although a plethora of writing exists on the impact of neoliberalism on African and other developing economies (Onyeonoru 2003; Fawole 2004; Mkandawire 2005), this study focuses on its impact on peacebuilding and state reconstruction in post-conflict West Africa.

As an ideology, neoliberalism is premised on a strong belief in promoting the 'public good' by following the principles of 'the free market and open competition,' 'limited state intervention and welfare,' 'individualistic self-interest,' 'rational utility-maximisation' and 'comparative advantage' of 'free trade' (Haque 1999:203). Although neoliberal advocates differ in the intensity of their belief in various neoliberal assumptions, all the proponents of this approach have certain predispositions in common. Their positions are also linked to the principles of neo-classical economics, although neoliberalism pays less attention to market failures (Colclough 1991:21).

However, central to all neoliberal thought is (i) an emphasis on 'the role of the market' and 'a minimalist role of the state' (Sargent 1990:97-9; Watson and Seddon 1994:170) (ii) advocacy of policies based on deregulation and privatisation (Fitzgerald 1988 and Haque 1996) (iii) emphasis on comparative advantage and opposition to protectionist policies for domestic industries (Colclough 1991:8-12) (iv) liberalisation of trade, facilitation of foreign investment and elimination of export controls and import licensing (Harvey 1991:138) and (v) opposition to economic development, poverty reduction through state intervention and other major objectives of structuralist thinking, and a simultaneous emphasis on economic growth, in some cases endorsing inequality as 'a prerequisite' for growth (Colclough 1991:6; King 1987:3). With these assumptions, neoliberalism takes on a global policy stance. Through the role of the International Monetary Fund (IMF) and the World Bank, it advocates 'the replacement of the developmental interventionist state' with 'a non-interventionist state' and encourages 'the expansion of market forces' through the implementation of market-friendly policies (Haque 1999:203; Watson and Seddon 1994:335-8).

Applied to post-conflict state reconstruction, neoliberalism is closely linked with international peacebuilding. Although peacebuilding has no rigid canonical definition (Doyle and Sambanis 2000:799), it refers to the 'actions undertaken at the end of a conflict to consolidate peace and prevent a recurrence of armed confrontation' (Annan 1998). The academic literature on international peace operations has expanded since the 1990s, when the United Nations launched a series of peacebuilding missions after the Cold War in Central America, Southeast Asia, Southeast Europe and sub-Saharan Africa. Several issues have been emphasised in the literature, including (i) the methods for dealing with civil conflicts and their humanitarian effects (ii) the role of democracies, economic interdependence and memberships of international organisations in reinforcing peaceful relations (Rummel 1997; Russett and Starr 2000; Hegre *et al.* 2001; Russett and Oneal 2001; Kim and Rousseau 2005; Bennett 2006; Souva and Prins 2006) (iii) the practical challenges of peacebuilding operations as well as (iv) the ideological assumptions underlying such operations. This expansive focus is understandable given the recent crises in the Congo, East Timor and Kosovo.

However, in spite of its achievements, the problem with neoliberal peacebuilding lies in the contradiction between its stated goals, the changes it brings about and the actual needs of war-torn societies. As often stated, neoliberal peacebuilding seeks to prevent the recurrence of violence in countries just emerging from civil conflicts. This goal has mostly been pursued through the deployment of peacebuilding missions to countries on the continent just emerging from civil wars – Angola, Mozambique, Namibia, Rwanda and Sierra Leone. In achieving this goal, post-conflict transformations have privileged a particular vision of how states should be internally reorganised based on the principles of liberal democracy and market-oriented economics. The UN and other influential agencies have supported the transformation of these states into liberal market democracies. Not only have these agencies helped these post-conflict states administer elections; they have also encouraged the development of societies based on pluralistic democracy and the rule of law (Paris 2002:637-9).

In the process, peacebuilders have transmitted standards of 'appropriate behaviour' from the Western liberal core of the international system to the failed states currently negotiating post-conflict transitions in the periphery. Beyond its stated goals, neoliberal peacebuilding thus translates into a rather benign version of what Roland Paris (2002:637) calls '*mission civilisatrice,*' which furthers the neocolonial belief in the role of imperial powers in civilising dependent regions of the world. While actual peace depends not only on liberal political and economic arrangements but also on a functioning state apparatus capable of upholding the rule of law and containing societal competition within peaceful bounds, given the operational constraints of the international normative environment (Paris 2003) neoliberal peacebuilding treats functioning state institutions as a given and wrongly focuses on the relationship between violent conflict and already constituted regimes (Paris 2006:425). This limitation underlines its inappropriateness for Africa's post-conflict situations.

Neoliberal peacebuilding has also proved ineffectual in stimulating economic development in post-conflict states, thus undermining the prospects for state consolidation (Barbara 2008:307-10). Although peacebuilding operations on the continent will undoubtedly continue to require international attention, the lessons of the past do not add up to a successful record of performance (Tschirgi 2004:i). One major obstacle undermining effective peacebuilding has been the failure of international actors to adapt their assistance to the political dynamics and other practical realities of the war-torn societies they seek to support. This disconnect has been manifested at conceptual, policy, operational and institutional levels. Conceptually, the very notion of 'post-conflict' is fraught with tensions as it wrongly assumes an end to conflict. As David Moore (2000:12) points out:

> ...the concept is caught up in tensions between neo-liberal and more interventionist visions of development in general. It is also implicated in contention over the resources allocated from the coffers of the advanced capitalist world to the rebuilding of war-torn societies on the periphery. More fundamentally, it is entangled in the complex nature of the causes of and cures for conflict in Africa.

Policy-wise, externally-driven peacebuilding projects err by adopting 'a one-size fits all' approach in negotiating peace in war-torn states. Most post-conflict rehabilitation programmes have been conducted with little critical self-reflection on the underlying assumptions and structural biases of the post-conflict peacebuilding efforts (Krause and Jutersonke 2005:447-50). The major reason for this shortcoming is the disconnect in the orientations of policymakers and practitioners between security priorities and the actual development needs of the societies in question. Institution-building has often been undertaken prematurely. This has added to the widespread discrepancy between the prescriptions made by various donors and the resources, which they often make available (Ottaway 2002:1001-15).

Ideologically, notwithstanding the growing consensus among scholars and policy analysts across the Global South, neoliberals have failed to acknowledge the many problems that have characterised the application of the Western model of the nation-state to post-crisis contexts across the world, especially in Africa. Given the World Bank's perception of war-torn societies as an alibi for creating 'market friendly opportunities on the level playing fields assumed by the "post-conflict" discourse' (Moore 2000:11), neoliberal state-building has rather compounded internal conflicts in Africa and their destabilising potential for neighbouring states by creating numerous ungoverned territories, which are capable of providing safe haven for terrorists (Obi 2006:1-6; Francois and Sud 2006:141-5).

Far from establishing 'developed' polities on the liberal democratic model through the restoration of 'political stability' in the process of this development, neoliberal peacebuilding has instead renewed the triple crisis of capitalist modernisation in Africa. 'Primitive accumulation,' 'nation-state formation' and 'democratisation' have remained largely uncompleted projects. As David Moore (2001:909) elaborates:

> Neoliberal globalisation simultaneously encourages these trends yet makes them difficult to resolve, given its anti-statism, its exclusionary version of democracy, and the violence inherent in the emergence of private property rights out of precapitalist modes of production that have been mediated by colonial and postcolonial institutions and the dynamics of the Cold War.

Above all, neoliberal promises for 'failed states' in Africa run up against a major contradiction, namely the structural impossibility of normal capitalist development – economic, political and social – in colonial and postcolonial societies (Chatterjee 1974:24). Thus, viewed in terms of democratic development and post-conflict peacebuilding, neoliberalism is ill-fated and can hardly engender social progress for failed states and other 'backward countries' of the world. According to Samir Amin (1989:5):

> The recent past is marked by global movements to democratize political regimes. In socialist countries, the movement forced regimes to take it into account, adopt (sic) to its exigencies or perish. Although it has not reached the same popular dimension, in third world capitalist countries, the demand for democracy signals a qualitative leap in the penetration of democratic consciousness. Simultaneously, one finds the rise of neo-liberalism, a generalised offensive aimed at the rehabilitation of the absolute superiority of private property, the legitimisation of social inequalities and anti-statism. Neo-liberalism has no frontiers. Orchestrated by an unprecedented media campaign it unilaterally asserts that 'the market' – a euphemism for capitalism – is the central axis to any 'development.' Democratisation is considered as the necessary and natural product of the submission to the rationality of the worldwide market. A simple double equation is deducible from this logic: capitalism = democracy, democracy = capitalism. The focus is on technical and scientific progress whereas the social realities which hide behind 'the market forces' are systematically occulted. The present offensive of Western countries 'in favour of democracy' is in fact an offensive against socialism. Similarly, 'national liberation' is proclaimed obsolete; 'nationalism' is accused of necessarily engendering a deadly delay in the international competition. There is no need to denigrate the heritage of Western bourgeois democracy. But the dominant contemporary perspective marked by Anglo-Saxon evolutionism and pragmatism empoverishes (sic) the debate by reducing democracy as a set of precise and limited rights and practices independent from the desired social perspectives.

In Sierra Leone, notwithstanding the return to democratic rule, obstacles abound, ranging from governance weaknesses in terms of capacity and domestic regulatory schemes for diamonds to the existence of illicit mining and the smuggling of diamonds to regional instability (Grant 2005:443-50).

While post-conflict elections have been widely expected to help consolidate the country's fragile peace and build legitimacy, legitimation is a function of good governance, which transcends the successful holding of competitive elections. Beyond the rituals that go with regime transitions, democratic governance entails critical considerations about how an elected government exercises power. The presence and institutionalisation of civil and political rights, the operation of a free press, the existence of an independent judiciary, vibrant associational life and a culture of mutual tolerance, the possibility of compromise and the accommodation of dissenting interests and views are all integral to democratisation and state viability (Kandeh 2003:190).

Although a few achievements have been recorded in Sierra Leone's democratic operations – the most notable being 'the peaceful alternation of the political parties in power through the ballot box in 2007,' a development that restored public confidence in elections as mechanisms of 'peaceful' political change – the country still confronts a number of challenges. These include the country's inability to tackle corruption, mass deprivation and the role of political parties as unreconstructed patronage institutions unresponsive to popular currents and mass aspirations (Kandey 2003:189; Kandey 2008:603-20). As Andrew Grant (2005:443-4) notes:

> As a result of more than a decade of civil conflict, much in the way of infrastructure has been destroyed, such as roads, bridges, hospitals, schools, electricity grids, communication links, housing and commercial enterprises. Notably, what little existed in terms of infrastructure before the outbreak of civil war was already in poor shape because of more than two decades of corruption and 'bad' governance ... The social damage inflicted by the civil war should not be underestimated. Though difficult to assess in monetary terms, the losses incurred by Sierra Leoneans as a result of death, torture, injury and displacement are substantial. Thus the scope and depth of post-conflict reconstruction must extend beyond the simple rebuilding of physical infrastructure.

In Nigeria, decades of misrule have undermined the emergence of an efficient bureaucratic state. They have also driven ethnic, religious and regional communities into developing sub-national conceptions of ethnic citizenship (Joseph 2003:159-65). As Frederick Cooper (2006:159) observes:

> During the struggles for independence, leaders of parties, trade unions, farmers' organisations, merchants' groups, students, and intellectuals aspired to a view of state-building with a strong 'civic' dimension: the state would act in the interest of citizens as a body, through institutions accessible to all. Once in power, African regimes proved distrustful of the very social linkages and the vision of citizenship on which they had ridden to power.

Instead of providing capital for diversifying and industrialising the Nigerian economy, oil revenues have mostly been used for political-elite patronage (Cooper 2006:173). Far from resolving the Niger Delta crisis, the Nigerian state intensifies it, while 'international interventionism' explores avenues for further accumulation through resource exploitation. While Nigeria's importance within and outside the continent can hardly be understated, numerous inter-group conflicts and the emergence of anti-state separatist formations and other challenges to nationhood indicate the absence of a legitimate and strong state in the country (Babawale 2002:379-83). The greatest weakness of externally driven peacebuilding projects in Africa is 'the limited attention focused on the state in such post-conflict settings.' This is a fundamental inadequacy. Our contention is that successful and enduring post-conflict peacebuilding and state reconstruction initiatives must focus on the state, while also advancing institutional and structural solutions to the root causes of conflicts from the bottom to the top. The rest of this study discusses Ake's intervention and contribution in this regard.

Reinventing the state in Africa: The contribution of Claude Ake

Ake did not use the concepts of 'peacebuilding' and 'state reconstruction' with reference to 'post-conflict Africa,' which are central to this study. Nor did his reflections and writings directly address the issue of 'reinventing the state in post-conflict Africa,' but they did illuminate the debate on the challenges confronting Africa in a post-Cold War world. Ake's writings at this time (1997) focused on the challenges posed to post-Cold War Africa by intra-state conflicts and crises, particularly those related to complex 'humanitarian emergencies.'

Although the continent recorded remarkable achievements in multiparty democratisation and economic reform (Young 2002:533), the significance of the 1990s for sub-Saharan Africa lies in 'the coincidence of the transformation in the international system with a profound internal crisis of the state in the continent' (Clapham 1997:99). Ake (1996 and 1997) analyses the implications of Africa's exploitation, marginalisation and poverty – driven by both local and global forces – for the conflicts and wars in the region. Although his works provide only limited coverage of 'peacebuilding' and 'state reconstruction' in 'post-conflict Africa,' which only took centre stage a few years before his sudden death in 1996, nevertheless, some of his contributions and insights can be linked to ongoing debates and reflections on 'peacebuilding' and 'state reconstruction' in 'post-conflict Africa.'

His major contribution in this regard relates to his critique of the state in Africa, especially the unique features of the state and their implications for the continent. He traced the history of the state in Africa to (i) colonialism and capitalist penetration, and (ii) the eventual political legacy of colonialism for the continent. And, following his 'limited autonomy thesis' and the characterisation of the 'social formations in Africa' as a colonial creation, Ake (1985a, 1985b and 1996) describes them as best understood as 'states in formation' and faults the process of 'state formation' on the continent. According to him, in spite of the formal independence of the state in Africa, the colonial character, inimical to development, still characterises the postcolonial state. Arguing that much is fundamentally wrong with the present composition of the state in Africa, he concludes that the state in Africa cannot deliver on the expectations of statehood unless it is fundamentally transformed.

Ake (1985b:4ff) argues that 'the rudimentary development of the state form in Africa' underlines the Hobbesian character of political struggles – usually based on relations of raw power among contending groups and social classes – in which right is co-extensive with power and security depends solely on the control of state power. This, he says, inhibits equality, formal freedom and competitive politics. It also undermines the legitimation of power – a problem underlying the crises of authority and nation-building on the continent – given the personalised use of the state's coercive resources.

Above all, the rudimentary development of the state form in Africa engenders 'the problem of contradictions and conflicts of the socio-economic formation.' The possibility of resolving contradictions is severely limited as the differences between groups in struggle are (mis)represented as absolute. These exacerbate 'the problem of political instability for which Africa is deservedly notorious' (Ake 1985b:5). In another account, Ake (1997:2) avers that:

> The state ... is burdened with onerous responsibilities which it is hardly in a position to fulfil. In particular, it is supposed to undertake economic development in the face of a weak or non-existent entrepreneurial class. Along with that daunting challenge, it is also expected to undertake state-building, nation-building and political integration. The problem is that these are tasks which presuppose the absence of the state or its rudimentary existence. Somewhat incongruously, a fledging state is expected to tame the anarchy of complex heterogeneities and their immanent centrifugalism when it is ludicrously weak. Quiet clearly, this is an improbable proposition.

As a way out of its current crises, Ake (1985a and 1985b) recommends the autochthonous transformation of the state as a recipe for improving its capacity and institutions. One approach to this is to rethink our understanding of colonialism and its legacies for the continent, the role of multinational capital, dependent capitalism, the centralisation of power as well as the impact of corrupt and authoritarian elites in Africa (Ake 1997). He presents democratisation as the most salient option for addressing the norm-less struggles over state power, ethnic conflict, resource wars and Africa's humanitarian emergencies.

In the context of Ake's reflections (1985a, 1985b and 1997), one understands the historic fault lines in Africa's experience with state formation. In this connection, the failure to transform the character of the state on the continent – in spite of formal political independence – engenders conflict over state power and the resources that access to state power offers. Ake harped insistently on 'now' as the temporal horizon for action, but far from being transcended; this failure is still very much with us. Twentieth century anti-colonial demands for self-rule in Africa achieved the vision of 'a quasi-independent state' but failed to transform the structures of the colonial state or imagine alternative conceptions of nationhood and statehood independent of the European model (Chakrabarty 2000:8).

The modern state has everywhere in Africa been patterned on the European model, with all its contradictions for the post-colony (Chatterjee 1993:14). Put differently, the historical patterns and global conditions which gave rise to the state in Africa have not been fundamentally altered (Cooper 2006:183). This is a major limitation of the nationalist response to the colonial intervention (Chatterjee 1993:34). It explains the continent's vulnerability to ideological and policy tinkering by neo-imperial brains trusts, with all their hard-nosed arguments on the lack of development in Africa. It also explains why the postcolonial state in its present form has been ineffectual, embattled and hounded into several reform programmes by the external donor community and international financial institutions (Young 2002:532-5). With neoliberalism, the wheel has only come full circle.

State-building in Africa therefore operates within the framework of a borrowed knowledge system whose representational structure corresponds to the very structure of power, which intellectual and nationalist leaders on the continent seek to repudiate (Chatterjee 1986). The anti-colonial vision has been influential throughout the postco-lonial world, instituting the foundations of modern critiques of socially unjust practices of caste, oppression of women, lack of rights for labouring and subaltern classes, and of colonialism itself (Chatterjee 1986:4; and Chakrabarty 2000:4). However, it has been ineffectual in erecting the foundations of an independent state free of neo-imperial dom-inance and capable of delivering on the expectations of a truly developmental state.

Thus, nationalism may have succeeded in liberating the nation from colonialism but not from the knowledge system of the West, which continues to dominate the continent. Through their opposition to colonialism, nationalist elites in Africa checked a specific political form of metropolitan capitalist dominance. Although they rejected the domi-nant rhetoric such as the civilising mission of the West – 'the white man's burden' – they ignored the need for an epistemological revolution in the Western knowledge system on which the operations of the state are premised (Chatterjee 1986). While the lessons of decolonisation and what it means for world history are irreversible, this failure explains the continued dominance of the continent by the knowledge system of the West in the postcolonial era.

Ake (1979, 1996a and 1997) establishes a connection between 'knowledge-produc-tion,' 'state-building' and 'development' on the continent, and bemoans the 'poverty of ideas' with which state-building has been undertaken since decolonisation. Put together, his works indicate that democratisation cannot ignore the character of the state. After all, the colonial state was not just the agency that brought the modular forms of the modern state to the colonies, it was also the agency destined never to fulfil its normalis-ing mission in the post-colony. And the postcolonial state throughout Africa and Asia has 'only expanded and not transformed the basic institutional arrangements of colonial law and administration, of the courts, the bureaucracy, the police, the army and the various technical services of government' (Chatterjee 1993:15; Thompson and Garratt 1934; Dutt 1947; Habib 1995).

Africa inherited the European system of government and administration in its origi-nal form based on 'imitated' constitutional principles, 'borrowed' technologies of power and administration, merely replacing the personnel. The elites of the 'new states' *could not think* of an entirely new system (Pylee 1967:15). Having replicated the Western model, 'the state in Africa' remains 'an imposed institution inappropriate to the condi-tions of Africa' (Cooper 2006:186). This way, decolonisation foreclosed other significant alternatives that were once at the centre of attention, such as supranational federations and pan-Africanism, and put in place a kind of state headed by a ruling class conscious of its own interests and fragility. The failure by successive regimes on the continent to see to the reality of change in this regard is what Frantz Fanon (1968:119-65) describes as 'the pitfalls of national consciousness.'

Conclusion

This paper has attempted a critique of externally driven state reconstruction projects in post-conflict West Africa. It has highlighted the limitations of the nationalist response to colonial intervention, and the ruinous impact of status quo elite politics for development and state transformation in Africa. Focusing on Sierra Leone and Nigeria's Niger Delta, it has drawn attention to the relevance of Ake's works for advancing an autochthonous intervention on the conditions for reinventing the state in post-conflict Africa. In critiquing neoliberal peacebuilding, this study is not breaking new ground. The limitations of state-reconstruction frameworks based on the neoliberal peace paradigm have been covered in the literature.

  While several studies have focused on the post-Cold War conflicts in Africa, few of these efforts have historicised the state in relation to such wars or linked them to the character of the state on the continent. Consequently, such works gloss over the need for state transformation as a prerequisite for sustainable peacebuilding in post-conflict societies. This study, drawing on Ake's seminal thinking, fills this gap and establishes the need to focus on the autochthonous transformation of the state as a central component of peacebuilding programmes in post-conflict contexts.

  How *else* does one account for the transformations taking place within the continent without engaging the state? Ake's focus on the state in Africa is by no means the only approach to understanding the conflicts and wars in the region. His argument regarding the limited autonomy of the state in Africa is also neither his only thesis nor his strongest position on the state in Africa. Rather, by relaying his argument on the state in Africa's limited autonomy, we have merely drawn attention to an instructive approach that we consider relevant to comprehending ongoing transformations on the continent. Far from limiting our analytical options, the aim has been to enrich and expand such options by highlighting salient features and other attributes of the state glossed over in extant literature on the state in Africa. One interesting outcome of recent debates on Orientalism and postcoloniality has been a renewal of interest in the intellectual history of colonial Africa.

  Theoretically, a major contribution by Ake to the understanding of political thought in Africa is the redirection of attention to the state, its character and unique features and their implications for conflicts and socioeconomic transformation on the continent. While Hegel, Marx, Engels, Lenin and more recently Poulantzas and Ralph Miliband have contributed significantly to our understanding the state in advanced capitalist societies in the West, Claude Ake, Hamza Alavi and Samir Amin are instructive voices in understanding its trajectory in Africa and other postcolonial societies. According to

Ake (1985a and 1996), the European model of the nation-state is the major institution engrafted by the 'core' on to the 'peripheries' in the form of 'the state in Africa.'

However, unlike the European model, which developed within Europe, the state in Africa is 'a force imposed on society from without.' This logical inversion of state formation in Africa underlines the alien-ness of the state in Africa – its lack of conformity with the expectations and practices of the people. This is what makes the state inadequate on the continent. In effect, while most of the state forms in precolonial Africa arguably approximated statehood – at least to the extent that they were developed within the indigenous societies in which they operated – the same is not true of the colonial and postcolonial state in Africa.

While the 'stateness' of the socioeconomic formations in Africa as systems of authority that monopolise the use of force over given territories is not in doubt, their 'autonomy,' 'autotchtoneity' and 'African-ness' are matters of continuing debate. For that reason, the descriptive referent 'the state in Africa' rather than 'the African state' is generally adopted in this study. The state's alien-ness is evident in its existence as a suspended power aloof and in abstraction from the society, mainly for the purpose of maintaining law and order and as a basis for maximising the political conditions of exploitation. This situation also explains the over-developed status of the state's apparatuses of violence relative to its education, health and welfare systems. Regrettably, local elites under successive regimes on the continent have demonstrated neither the will nor the discipline to transform these inherited structures of the state.

Following Ake, one understands the contradictory effects of global capitalism and its connections with new forms of empire, governmentality and violence. He insists that we recognise the insufficiency of dominant categories of analysis that all too often are aseptic and anodyne. Old models of citizenship, empire and the state have thus become anachronisms. In Ake's view, new models – especially those of autochthonous transformation of the state based on endogenous knowledge-production – now fire our analytical and political imagination of the state. The trajectory of state formation in Africa, as elsewhere in the Global South, does not conform to the known experience in the West. The task of empirical research and, indeed, political theory is not to dismiss this interesting contrast, but to explain it and establish its implications for how society is constituted in the region. Although the rise of mass politics in 20th century Africa has led to the development of new techniques of governing population groups, the proliferation of security and welfare technologies has created modern governmental bodies that administer populations but do not provide citizens with an arena for democratic deliberation.

Under these conditions, multiparty democracy is no longer 'government of the people, by the people and for the people.' It has rather become a world of power whose startling dimensions and unwritten rules deny the expectations of the voiceless mass of the dominated populations. Such politics, especially as operated outside the traditionally defined arena of civil society and the formal legal institutions of the modern state, engenders the tensions that underlie conflicts and wars. Ake considers the global conditions within which such local forms of popular politics – based on conflict and war – have not only appeared but transformed both community violence and global society.

In reinventing the state in Africa, Ake charges us to engage the epistemological bases of state-building and state formation from the perspective of knowledge-production. This, according to him, is mainly because ideological control and exploitation of the continent have been achieved, for the most part, through the continent's dependence on the West in the sphere of knowledge. The hegemonic status of European historiography has contributed to a longstanding neglect of knowledge produced from the Global South (Holsinger 2002): hence the series of interventions across the different disciplines, localised and bound by their own historically produced rules of formation but thematically connected by their convergence on the 'the state,' the most contested concept in the post-colony. While several efforts have been made to transcend the knowledge systems of Europe, a persistent contradiction has been the assertion of an inseparable complicity between this borrowed knowledge and its epistemic privileging over other local and often incommensurable knowledge.

While acknowledging the role of external influences, notably the legacies of colonialism, the impact of the Cold War and contemporary global politics (Falola 2002), this study has underlined the failure by intellectual and nationalist elites to transform the state, and the implications of such failings not just for conflict, but also the programmed exclusion of Africa from the beneficial proceeds of global capitalism.

Africa's dependence in the sphere of knowledge has serious implications for the untransformed character of the state, the spread of conflict and the continent's lack of development. It is the failure to imagine alternative forms of the modern state independent of the European model that underpins Africa's continued dependence on the West for 'inspiration' and 'solutions' to its problems. This also underlies the interventionist basis of neoliberalism and other foreign recipes, which are not helpful to the continent. Far from being autochthonous, state-building and knowledge-production in Africa operate within a borrowed context (Kaviraj and Khilnani 2001). 'The knowledge of backwardness is never very comforting' (Chatterjee 1986:6). 'It is even more disturbing when its removal requires coming to terms with an alien culture.' State-transformation is an urgent task on Africa's agenda, and the question of 'Africanising the state' through endogenous knowledge-production is critical in this regard. Crucial considerations for Africa include (i) what kind of state should be constructed (ii) what kinds of relationships should be forged across state lines and (iii) what kinds of recognition within states should be given to the affinities to which the citizens subscribe (Cooper 2006:186).

Although the restoration of their states' capacities is a critical component of the democratic order, Nigeria, Sierra Leone and other post-conflict states must work towards the progressive transformation of their governance and public administrations with a view to rekindling socioeconomic development. The political processes in these states should also be reconstituted in a manner that genuinely engages and incorporates their citizens in the state relegitimation process. While their overall frameworks remain largely based on imitations developed in the West, efforts should be made to endogenise these states by evoking innovative practices at the local level. It is important to think of means of transcending the legacies of the colonial past. The one-sided reference to the 'colonial past' in the unmaking of Africa's present and future histories is flawed. By focusing 'exclusively' on the role of external actors, Africans wrongly absolve themselves of their failings and are reduced to the typical colonial role of helpless victims and chronically dependent actors, lacking the capacity for appropriate agency both to transform the state and redress the historic structures underlying the reproduction of crisis on the continent.

References

Adejumobi, S., 2001, 'Citizenship, rights and the problems of conflicts and civil wars in,' Africa. *Human Rights Quarterly* 23(1):148-70.

Africa Action, 2003, 'Africa policy for a new era: Ending segregation in US foreign relations.' January: www.africaaction.org/featdocs/afr2003.htm.

Agbaje, A.A.B., 1991, 'Review: Quarantine for the African state?' *Journal of Modern African Studies* 29(4):723-7.

Ali, A.G.A., 2000, 'The economics of conflicts in Africa: An overview,' *Journal of African Economies* 9(3):235-43.

Ake, C., 1967a, *A theory of political integration*. Homewood, IL: Dorsey Press.

—, 1967b, 'Political integration and political stability: A hypothesis,' *World Politics* 19(3):486-99.

—, 1973, 'Explaining political instability in new states,' *Journal of Modern African Studies* 11(3):347-59.

—, 1974. Modernisation and political instability: A theoretical exploration. *World Politics* 26(4):576-91.

—, 1979, *Social science as imperialism*: *The theory of political development*. Ibadan: Ibadan University Press.

—, 1981, *A political economy of Africa*. London: Longman.

—, 1982, 'The state of the nation: Intimations of disaster. Presidential address to the Nigerian Political Science Association (NPSA).' Port Harcourt: Nigerian Political Science Association.

—, 1985a, 'The future of the state in Africa,' *International Political Science Review* 6(1):105-14.

—, 1985b, (ed.), *The political economy of Nigeria*. Lagos and London: Longman.

—, 1985c, 'Why is Africa not developing?' *West Africa*, 17 June.

—, 1996a, *Democracy and development in Africa*. Washington DC: The Brookings Institution.

—, 1996b, 'Shelling Nigeria ablaze,' *Tell Newsmagazine*, 29 January.

—, 1997, *Why humanitarian emergencies occur*: *Insights from the interface of state, democracy and civil society*. Helsinki: United Nations University-World Institute for Development Economic Research. Research for Action 31.

— ,2000, *The feasibility of democracy in Africa*. Dakar: CODESRIA.

Allen, C., 1999, 'Warfare, endemic violence and state collapse in Africa,' *Review of African Political Economy* 81(1):367-84.

Amin, S., 1989, 'La question democratique dans le tiers monde contemporain,' *Africa Development* 14(2):5-25.

—, 1990, *Maldevelopment*: *Anatomy of a global failure*. London and New Jersey: Zed Books.

—, 1991, 'The state and development,' in Held, D. (ed.), *Political theory today*. Stanford: Stanford University Press.

Annan, K., 1998, 'The causes of conflict and the promotion of durable peace and sustainable development in Africa.' Report of the Secretary-General to the Security Council, S/1998/318 (13 April 1998).

Arowosegbe, J.O., 2008, 'Decolonizing the social sciences in the global south: Claude Ake and the praxis of knowledge-production in Africa.' *Working Paper* 79. Leiden: African Studies Centre.

—, 2010, 'The state, democracy and development in the works of Claude Ake.' Unpublished PhD thesis. Ibadan: University of Ibadan.

Babawale, T., 2002, 'The challenges of nationhood,' in Falola, T. (ed.), *Nigeria in the twentieth century*. Durham NC: Carolina Academic Press.

Baker, B., 2006, 'The African post-conflict policing agenda in Sierra Leone,' *Conflict, Security and Development* 6 (1):25-49.

Bangura, Y., 1992, 'Authoritarian rule and democracy in Africa: A theoretical discourse, in Rudebeck, L. (ed.), *When democracy makes sense*: *studies in the democratic potential of third world popular movements*. Uppsala: AKUT.

Barbara, J., 2008, 'Rethinking neo-liberal state building: Building post-conflict development states,' *Development in Practice* 18(3):307-18.

Barnes, S., 2005, 'Global flows: Terror, oil and strategic philanthropy,' *African Studies Review* 48(1):1-23.

Basedau, M., 2005, 'Context matters: Rethinking the resource curse in sub-Saharan Africa.' *Working Paper 1*. Hamburg: Institute of African Affairs.

Bennett, D.S., 2006, 'Toward a continuous specification of the democracy-autocracy connection,' *International Studies Quarterly* 50(1):313-38.

Boesen, J. *et al.* 1986 (eds), *Tanzania*: *crisis and struggle for survival*. Uppsala: Scandinavian Institute of African Studies.

Bratton, M. and R. Mattes. 2004. What the people say about the reforms. In Gyimah-Boadi, E. (ed.): *Democratic reforms in Africa*: *The quality of progress*. Boulder CO: Lynne Rienner.

Callaghy, T. and J. Ravenhill (eds), 1993, *Hemmed in*: *Responses to Africa's economic crisis*. New York: Columbia University Press.

Callaghy, T., 1994, 'Africa: Back to the future,' *Journal of Democracy* 5(4):133-45.

Chabal, P. and J. P. Daloz, 1999, *Africa works*: *Disorder as political instrument*. Oxford: James Currey.

Chakrabarty, D., 2000, *Provincializing Europe*: *Post-colonial thought and historical difference*. Princeton and Oxford: Princeton University Press.

Chatterjee, P., 1974, 'Modern American political theory with reference to underdeveloped nations,' *Social Scientists* 2 (12):24-42.

—, 1986, *Nationalist thought and the colonial world*: *a derivative discourse*. London: Zed Books.

—, 1993, *The nation and its fragments*: *Colonial and post-colonial histories*. Princeton, NJ: Princeton University Press.

—, 2004, *The politics of the governed*: *Reflections on popular politics in most of the world*. Oxford and New Delhi: Permanent Black.

Chege, M., 1995, 'Between Africa's extremes,' *Journal of Democracy* 6 (1).

Cheeseman, N., 2006, 'Introduction: Political linkage and political space in the era of decolonisation,' *Africa Today* 53(2):3-24.

Cheru, F., 2008, 'Foreword,' in Zack-Williams, A.B. (ed.), *The quest for sustainable development and peace*: *The 2007 Sierra Leone elections*. Policy Dialogue 2. Uppsala: Nordic Africa Institute.

Clapham, C., 1997, 'International relations in Africa after the Cold War.,' in Hale W. and E. Kienle (eds), *After the Cold War*: *Security and democracy in Africa and Asia*. London and New York: Tauris Academic Studies.

—, 1998, (ed.), *African guerrillas*. Oxford: James Currey.

Coleman, J.S., 1955, 'The problem of political integration in emergent Africa,' *Western Political Quarterly* 8(1):44-57.

Collier, P., 1999, 'On the economic consequences of civil war,' *Oxford Economic Papers* 51(1):168-83.

Colclough, C., 1991, 'Structuralism versus neo-liberalism: an introduction,' in Colclough, C. and J. Manor (eds), *States or markets? Neo-liberalism and the development policy debate*. New York: Oxford University Press.

Cooper, F., 2006, *Africa since 1940*: *The past of the present*. Cambridge: Cambridge University Press.

Davidson, B. and B. Munslow, 1990, 'The crisis of the nation-state in Africa,' *Review of African Political Economy* 17(49):9-21.

David-West, T., 1994, 'Yakassai's blackmail,' *Tell,* 31 January.

De Waal, A., 2003, 'How will HIV/AIDS transform African governance?' *African Affairs* 102(406):1-24.

De Walle, N.V., 2001, *African economies and the politics of permanent crisis, 1979-1999*. Cambridge: Cambridge University Press.

Deutsch, K., 1961, 'Social mobilisation and political development,' *American Political Science Review* 55(3):493-514.

Deutsch, K. (ed.), 1963, *Nation-Building*. New York: Atherton Press.

Dossa, S., 1998, 'Book review.' Martin Doornbos and Sudipta Kaviraj (eds),1997, *Dynamics of state formation*: *India and Europe compared*. New Delhi: Sage Publications.

Doyle, M.W. and N. Sambanis, 2000, 'International peace-building: A theoretical and quantitative analysism,' *American Political Science Review* 94(4).

Dutt, R.P., 1947, *India to-day*. Calcutta: Manisha.

Elbadawi, I. and N. Sambanis, 2000, 'Why are there so many civil wars in Africa? Understanding and preventing violent conflict,' *Journal of African Economies* 9(3):244-69.

Ebel, R., 2004, 'Crafting a US energy policy for Africa,' in *Release of the Africa policy advisory panel report*. CSIS July 8: www.csis.org/africa/sarah.htm.

Efemini, A.O., 2000, *Claude Ake's philosophy of development*: *Implications for Nigeria*. Port Harcourt: University of Port Harcourt Press.

Ejobowah, J.B., 2000, 'Who owns the oil? The politics of ethnicity in the Niger Delta of Nigeria,' *Africa Today* 47(1):29-47.

Ellis, S.D.K., 1996, 'Africa after the Cold War: New patterns of government and politics,' *Development and Change* 27(1):1-28.

—, 2002, 'Writing histories of contemporary Africa,' *Journal of African History* 43(1):1-26.

Escobar, A., 1995, *Encountering development*: *The making and unmaking of the third world*. Princeton NJ: Princeton University Press.

Falola, T., 2002 (ed.), *Nigeria in the twentieth century*. Durham NC: Carolina Academic Press.

Fanon, F., 1968, *The wretched of the earth*. New York: Grove Press.

Fawole, W.A., 2004, 'A continent in crisis: Internal conflicts and external interventions in Africa,' *African Affairs* 103:297-303.

Finer, S.E., 1974, 'The man on horseback,' *Armed Forces and Society* 1(1):5-27.

Fitzgerald, R., 1988, *When government goes private*: *Successful alternatives to public services*. New York: Universe Books.

Francois, M. and I. Sud, 2006, 'Promoting stability and development in fragile and failed states,' *Development Policy Review* 24(2):141-60.

Frank, A.G., 1981, *Crisis in the third world*. London: Heinemann.

Furnivall, J.S., 1939, *Netherlands India*. Cambridge: Cambridge University Press.

—, 1942, 'The political economy of the tropical Far East,' *Journal of the Royal Central Asiatic Society* 29:195-210.

—, 1945, 'Some problems of tropical economy,' in Hinden, R. (ed.), *Fabian colonial essays*. London: George Allen and Unwin.

Ghai, D., 2000 (ed.), *Renewing social and economic progress in Africa*. Basingstoke and London: Macmillan.

Goldwyn, D.L. and J.S. Morrison, 2004, 'Promoting transparency in the African oil sector: A report of the CSIS task force on rising US energy stakes in Africa.' CSIS March: www.csis.org/africa/index.htm#oil.

Graf, W., 1988, *The Nigerian state*. London: James Currey.

Grant, A.J., 2005, 'Diamonds, foreign aid and the uncertain prospects for post-conflict reconstruction in Sierra Leone,' *The Round Table* 94(381):443-57.

Guerrero, A. and R. Barragan, 2003, 'The spirit of Bolivian laws: Citizenship, infamy and patriarchal hierarchy,' in Pandey, G. and P. Geschiere (eds), *The forging of nationhood*. New Delhi and Amsterdam: Manohar and SEPHIS.

Gutkind, P.C.W. and I. Wallerstein, 1976 (eds), *The political economy of contemporary Africa*. Beverly Hills and London: Sage Publications.

Habib, I., 1995, *Essays in Indian history*: *Towards a Marxist perception*. New Delhi: Tulika.

Hale, W. and E. Kienle, 1997 (eds), *After the Cold War*: *Security and democracy in Africa and Asia*. London and New York: Tauris Academic Studies.

Harneit-Sievers, A., 2006, *Constructions of belonging*: *Igbo communities and the Nigerian state in the twentieth century*. Rochester NY: University of Rochester Press.

Harris, K., 2005, 'Still relevant: Claude Ake's challenge to mainstream discourse on African politics and development,' *Journal of Third World Studies* 22(2):73-88.

Harvey, C., 1991, 'Recovery from macro-economic disaster in sub-Saharan Africa,' in Colclough C. and J. Manor (eds), *States or markets? Neo-liberalism and the development policy debate*. New York: Oxford University Press.

Haque, S.M., 1996, 'Public service under challenge in the age of privatisation,' *Governance: An International Journal of Policy and Administration* 9(2):186-216.

—, 1999, 'The fate of sustainable development under neo-liberal regimes in Developing countries,' *International Political Science Review* 20(2):197-218.

Hegre, H. *et al.*, 2001, 'Toward a democratic civil peace? Democracy, political change and civil war, 1816-1992,' *American Political Science Review* 95(1):33-48.

Held, D., 1985, 'Introduction: Central perspectives on the modern state,' in Held, D. *et al.* (eds), *States and societies*. Oxford: Blackwell in association with The Open University.

Herbst, J., 2000, 'Economic incentives, natural resources and conflict in Africa,' *Journal of African Economies* 9(3):270-94.

Hoffman, D., 2006, 'Disagreement: Dissent politics and the war in Sierra Leone,' *Africa Today* 52(3):3-22.

Holsinger, B.W., 2002, 'Medieval studies, post-colonial studies and the genealogies of critique,' *Speculum* 77(4):1195-227.

Ibeanu, O.O., 1993, 'The state and the market: Reflections on Ake's analysis of the state in the periphery,' *Africa Development* 18(3):117-31.

Ibrahim, J., 2006, *Transforming elections in West Africa into opportunities for political choice*. Occasional Electronic Paper 2.Uppsala: Nordic Africa Institute.

Isaacman, A., 2003, 'Legacies of engagement: Scholarship informed by political commitment,' *African Studies Review* 46(1):1-41.

Ismail, O., 2008, 'Power elites, war and postwar reconstruction in Africa: Continuities, discontinuities and paradoxes,' *Journal of Contemporary African Studies* 26(3):259-78.

Jackson, R.H. and C.G. Rosberg, 1982, 'Why Africa's weak states persist: The empirical and the juridical in statehood,' *World Politics* 35(1):1-24.

Jalee, P., 1977, *How capitalism works*. New York and London: Monthly Review Press.

Joseph, R., 2003, 'Africa: States in crisis,' *Journal of Democracy* 14(3):159-70.

Kandey, J.D., 1996, 'What does the 'militariat' do when it rules? Military regimes: The Gambia, Sierra Leone and Liberia,' *Review of African Political Economy* 23(69):387-404.

—, 1999, 'Ransoming the state: elite origins of subaltern terror in Sierra Leone,' *Review of African Political Economy* 26(81):349-66.

—, 2003, 'Sierra Leone's post-conflict elections of 2002,' *Journal of Modern African Studies* 41(2):189-216.

—, 2008, 'Rogue incumbents, donor assistance and Sierra Leone's second post-conflict elections of 2007,' *Journal of Modern African Studies* 46(4):603-635.

The Kaiama Declaration, 1998, <www.ijawcenter.com/kaiamadeclaration.html>, accessed 14 April 2005.

Kaviraj, S. and S. Khilnani, 2001 (eds), *Civil society: history and possibilities*. Cambridge: Cambridge University Press.

Kim, H.M. and D.L. Rousseau, 2005, 'The classical liberals were half right (or half wrong): New tests of the 'liberal peace,' 1960-1988,' *Journal of Peace Research* 42(1):523-43.

King, D.S., 1987, *The new left: Politics, markets and citizenship*. Chicago: Dorsey Press.

King, G. and L. Zeng, 2001, 'Improving forecasts of state failure,' *World Politics* 53(4):623-58.

Kothari, R., 1997, 'The agony of the modern state,' in Rahnema, M. and V. Bawtree (eds), *The post-development reader*. London: Zed Books.

Krause, K. and O. Jutersonke, 2005, 'Peace, security and development in post-conflict environments,' *Security Dialogue* 36(4):447-62.

Lancaster, C., 1999, *Aid to Africa*: *So much to do, so little time*. Chicago: University of Chicago Press.

Lewis, P.M., 1996, 'Economic reform and political transition in Africa: The quest for a politics of development,' *World Politics* 49(1):92-129.

Lijphart, A., 1971, 'Cultural diversity and theories of political integration,' *Canadian Journal of Political Science* 4(1):1-14.

Mama, A., 2007, 'Is it ethical to study Africa? Preliminary thoughts on scholarship and freedom,' *African Studies Review* 50(1):1-26.

Mamdani, M., 2003, 'From conquest to consent as the basis of state formation: Reflections on Rwanda,' in Pandey, G. and P. Geschiere (eds), *The forging of nationhood*. New Delhi and Amsterdam: Manohar and SEPHIS.

Mafeje, A.B.M., 1997, 'Democracy and development in Africa: A tribute to Claude Ake,' *African Journal of International Affairs* 1(1):1-17.

Martin, G., 1998, 'Reflections on democracy and development: The intellectual legacy of Claude Ake,' *Ufahamu* 26(1):102-9.

Mbembe, A., 2001, *On the postcolony*. Berkeley: University of California Press.

Milliken, J. and K. Krause, 2002, 'State failure, state collapse and state-reconstruction: Concepts, lessons and strategies,' *Development and Change* 33(5):753-74.

Mkandawire, T., 2002, 'The terrible toll of postcolonial "rebel movements" in Africa: Towards an explanation of the violence against the peasantry,' *Journal of Modern African Studies* 40(2):181-215.

—, 2005, 'Maladjusted African economies and globalisation,' *Africa Development* 30(1 and 2):1-33.

Moore, D., 2000, 'Levelling the playing fields and embedding illusions: "Post-conflict" discourse and neo-liberal "development" in war-torn Africa,' *Review of African Political Economy* 27(83):11-28.

—, 2001, 'Neo-liberal globalisation and the triple crisis of "modernisation" in Africa: Zimbabwe, the Democratic Republic of Congo and South Africa,' *Third World Quarterly* 22(6):909-29.

Mustapha, A.R., 2003, 'Transformation of minority identities in postcolonial Nigeria,' in Jega, A. (ed.), *Identity transformation and identity politics under structural adjustment in Nigeria*. Uppsala and Kano: Nordic Africa Institute and the Centre for Research and Documentation.

Nabudere, D.W., 2004, *Africa's First World War*: *Mineral wealth, conflicts and war in the great lakes region*. Pretoria: African Association of Political Science. AAPS Occasional Paper Series 8(1):1-113.

Nigeria, 1958, *Report of the commission appointed to enquire into the fears of minorities and the means of allaying them*. London: HMSO.

Nzongola-Ntalaja, G., 2006, 'Challenges to state building in Africa,' *African Identities* 4(1):71-88.

Obi, C.I., 1999, 'Resources, population and conflicts: Two African case studies,' *Africa Development* 24(3 and 4):47-69.

—, 2006, 'Terrorism in West Africa: Real, emerging or imagined threats?' *African Security Review* 15(3):87-101.

—, 2007, 'Introduction: Elections and the challenges of post-conflict democratisation in West Africa,' *African Journal of International Affairs* 10(1 and 2):1-11.

Ogoni Bill of Rights, 1990, 'Presented to the government and people of Nigeria.' <www.waado.org/NigerDelta/Rights/Declaration/Ogoni.html> 14 April 2005.

Olukoshi, A.O., 1993 (ed), *The politics of structural adjustment in Nigeria*. London: James Currey; Portsmouth NH: Heinemann Educational.

Onyeonoru, I., 2003, 'Globalisation and industrial performance in Nigeria,' *Africa Development* 28(3 and 4):36-66.

Osaghae, E.E., 1989, 'The character of the state, legitimacy crisis and social mobilisation in Africa: An explanation of form and character,' *Africa Development* 14(2):27-47.

—, 1991, 'Ethnic minorities and federalism in Nigeria,' *African Affairs* 90(359):237-58.

—, 1994, *Ethnicity and its management in Africa: The democratisation link*. Lagos and Port Harcourt: Malthouse Press.

—, 2005, 'The state of Africa's second liberation,' *Interventions: International Journal of Postcolonial Studies* 7(1):1-20.

Ottaway, M., 2002, 'Rebuilding state institutions in collapsed states,' *Development and Change* 33(5):1001-23.

—, 2003, 'Promoting democracy after conflict: The difficult choices,' *International Studies Perspectives* 4(1):314-22.

Pandey, G. and P. Geschiere, 2003, 'The forging of nationhood: The contest of citizenship, ethnicity and history,' in Pandey, G. and P. Geschiere (eds), *The forging of nationhood*. New Delhi and Amsterdam: Manohar and SEPHIS.

Paris, R., 2002a, 'Kosovo and the metaphor war,' *Political Science Quarterly* 117(3):423-50.

—, 2002b, 'International peacebuilding and the "mission civilisatrice",' *Review of International Studies* 28(1):637-57.

—, 2003, 'Peace-keeping and the constraints of global culture,' *European Journal of International Relations* 9(3):441-73.

—, 2006, 'Bringing the leviathan back in: Classical versus contemporary studies of the liberal peace,' *International Studies Review* 8(1):425-40.

Post, K. and M. Vickers, 1973, *Structure and conflict in Nigeria*. London: Heinemann.

Poulantzas, N., 1978, *State, power, socialism*. London: New Left Books and Sheed and Ward.

Pylee, M.V., 1967, *Constitutional history of India: 1600-1950*. Bombay: Apt Books.

Renoir, M., 2002, 'Breaking the link between resources and repression,' in The World Watch Institute, *State of the world 2002*. New York: W.W. Norton.

Ross, M.L., 2001, 'Does oil hinder democracy?' *World Politics* 53(3):325-61.

Rostow, W.W., 1961, *The stages of economic growth: A non-communist manifesto*. Cambridge: Cambridge University Press.

Rummel, R.J., 1997, *Power kills: Democracy as a method of non-violence*. New Brunswick: Transaction.

Russett, B. and J.R. Oneal, 2001, *Triangulating peace: Democracy, interdependence and international organisations*. New York: W.W. Norton.

Russett, B. and H. Starr, 2000, 'From democratic peace to Kantian peace: Democracy and conflict in the international system,' in Midlarsky, M.I. (ed.), *Handbook of War Studies II*. Ann Arbor: University of Michigan Press.

Sargent, L.T., 1990, *Contemporary political ideologies: A comparative analysis*. Pacific Grove CA: Brook/Cole Publishing.

Sawyer, A., 2004, 'Violent conflicts and governance challenges in West Africa: The case of the Mano River basin area,' *Journal of Modern African Studies* 42(3):437-63.

Silberfein, M., 2004, 'The geopolitics of conflict and diamonds in Sierra Leone,' *Geopolitics* 9(1):213-41.

Slater, D., 1998, 'Post-colonial questions for global times,' *Review of International Political Economy* 5(4):647-78.

Somjee, A.H., 1984, *Political society in developing countries*. London and Basingstoke: Macmillan.

Southall, A., 1974, 'State formation in Africa,' *Annual Review of Anthropology* 3(1):153-65.

Souva, M. and B. Prins, 2006, 'The liberal peace re-visited: The role of democracy, dependency and development in militarized interstate dispute initiation, 1950-1999,' *International Interactions* 32(1).

Suberu, R.T., 2004, 'Dilemmas of federalism.,' in Amoretti, U. and N. Bermeo (eds), *Federalism and territorial cleavages*. Baltimore and London: Johns Hopkins University Press.

—, 2008, 'The Supreme Court and federalism in Nigeria,' *Journal of Modern African Studies* 46(3):451-85.

Syed, A.H., 1980, 'The idea of a Pakistani nationhood,' *Polity* 12(4):575-97.

Thompson, E. and G.T. Garratt, 1934, *Rise and fulfilment of British rule in India*. Allahabad: Central Book Depot.

Thomson, A., 2000, *An introduction to African politics*. London and New York: Routledge.

The Times of India, 2007, 'India more stable than China and Russia,' Nagpur, 20 June.

Tschirgi, N., 2004, *Post-conflict peace-building revisited: Achievements, limitations and challenges*. New York: International Peace Academy.

Uche, C., 2008, 'Oil, British interests and the Nigerian civil war,' *Journal of African History* 49(1):111-35.

Ukiwo, U., 2007, 'From "pirates" to "militants": a historical perspective on anti-state and anti-oil company mobilisation among the Ijaw of Warri, western Niger Delta,' *African Affairs* 106(425):587-610.

United States Department of Commerce, 2004, 'International Trade Administration. US-African trade profile.' April.

United States Department of Energy, 2004, 'Energy Information Administration. Country analysis brief: Africa.' November.

Watson, J. and D. Seddon, 1994, *Free markets and food riots: The politics of global adjustment.* Cambridge MA: Blackwell.

Welch, C., 1983, 'Military disengagement from politics: Lessons from West Africa,' *Armed Forces and Society* 9(4):542-54.

Williams, G., 1980, *State and society in Nigeria.* Idanre: Afrografika.

Wilson, J.A. and D. Dalton, 1982, *The states of South-Asia: Problems of national integration.* New Delhi: Vikas Publishing House.

Wriggins, H.W., 1961, 'Impediments to unity in the new states: The case of Ceylon,' *American Political Science Review* 55(1):313-20.

The World Watch Institute, 2002, *State of the world 2002.* New York: W.W. Norton.

Young, C., 2002, 'Deciphering disorder in Africa: Is identity the key?' *World Politics* 54(4):532-57.

—, 2004, 'The end of the post-colonial state in Africa? Reflections on changing African political dynamics,' *African Affairs* 103(410):23-49.

Zack-Williams, A.B. (ed.), 2008, *The quest for sustainable development and peace: The 2007 Sierra Leone elections.* Policy Dialogue 2.Uppsala: Nordic Africa Institute.

Zartman, W.I. (ed.), 1995, *Collapsed states: The disintegration and restoration of legitimate authority.* Boulder CO: Lynne Rienner.

Zeleza, P.T., 1997, *Manufacturing African studies and crises.* Dakar: CODESRIA.

—, 2003, *Rethinking Africa's globalisation: The intellectual challenges.* Trenton NJ: World Press.

DISCUSSION PAPERS PUBLISHED BY THE INSTITUTE

Recent issues in the series are available electronically for download free of charge
www.nai.uu.se

1. Kenneth Hermele and Bertil Odén, *Sanctions and Dilemmas. Some Implications of Economic Sanctions against South Africa.*
    1988. 43 pp. ISBN 91-7106-286-6

2. Elling Njål Tjönneland, *Pax Pretoriana. The Fall of Apartheid and the Politics of Regional Destabilisation.*
    1989. 31 pp. ISBN 91-7106-292-0

3. Hans Gustafsson, Bertil Odén and Andreas Tegen, *South African Minerals. An Analysis of Western Dependence.*
    1990. 47 pp. ISBN 91-7106-307-2

4. Bertil Egerö, *South African Bantustans. From Dumping Grounds to Battlefronts.*
    1991. 46 pp. ISBN 91-7106-315-3

5. Carlos Lopes, *Enough is Enough! For an Alternative Diagnosis of the African Crisis.*
    1994. 38 pp. ISBN 91-7106-347-1

6. Annika Dahlberg, *Contesting Views and Changing Paradigms.*
    1994. 59 pp. ISBN 91-7106-357-9

7. Bertil Odén, *Southern African Futures. Critical Factors for Regional Development in Southern Africa.*
    1996. 35 pp. ISBN 91-7106-392-7

8. Colin Leys and Mahmood Mamdani, *Crisis and Reconstruction – African Perspectives.*
    1997. 26 pp. ISBN 91-7106-417-6

9. Gudrun Dahl, *Responsibility and Partnership in Swedish Aid Discourse.*
    2001. 30 pp. ISBN 91-7106-473-7

10. Henning Melber and Christopher Saunders, *Transition in Southern Africa – Comparative Aspects.*
    2001. 28 pp. ISBN 91-7106-480-X

11. *Regionalism and Regional Integration in Africa.*
    2001. 74 pp. ISBN 91-7106-484-2

12. Souleymane Bachir Diagne, et al., *Identity and Beyond: Rethinking Africanity.*
    2001. 33 pp. ISBN 91-7106-487-7

13. Georges Nzongola-Ntalaja, et al., *Africa in the New Millennium.* Edited by Raymond Suttner.
    2001. 53 pp. ISBN 91-7106-488-5

14. *Zimbabwe's Presidential Elections 2002.* Edited by Henning Melber.
    2002. 88 pp. ISBN 91-7106-490-7

15. Birgit Brock-Utne, *Language, Education and Democracy in Africa.*
    2002. 47 pp. ISBN 91-7106-491-5

16. Henning Melber et al., *The New Partnership for Africa's Development (NEPAD).*
    2002. 36 pp. ISBN 91-7106-492-3

17. Juma Okuku, *Ethnicity, State Power and the Democratisation Process in Uganda.*
    2002. 42 pp. ISBN 91-7106-493-1

18. Yul Derek Davids, et al., *Measuring Democracy and Human Rights in Southern Africa.* Compiled by Henning Melber.
    2002. 50 pp. ISBN 91-7106-497-4

19. Michael Neocosmos, Raymond Suttner and Ian Taylor, *Political Cultures in Democratic South Africa.* Compiled by Henning Melber.
    2002. 52 pp. ISBN 91-7106-498-2

20. Martin Legassick, *Armed Struggle and Democracy. The Case of South Africa.*
    2002. 53 pp. ISBN 91-7106-504-0

21. Reinhart Kössler, Henning Melber and Per Strand, *Development from Below. A Namibian Case Study.*
    2003. 32 pp. ISBN 91-7106-507-5

22. Fred Hendricks, *Fault-Lines in South African Democracy. Continuing Crises of Inequality and Injustice.*
    2003. 32 pp. ISBN 91-7106-508-3

23. Kenneth Good, *Bushmen and Diamonds. (Un)Civil Society in Botswana.*
    2003. 39 pp. ISBN 91-7106-520-2

24. Robert Kappel, Andreas Mehler, Henning Melber and Anders Danielson, *Structural Stability in an African Context.*
    2003. 55 pp. ISBN 91-7106-521-0

25. Patrick Bond, *South Africa and Global Apartheid. Continental and International Policies and Politics.*
    2004. 45 pp. ISBN 91-7106-523-7

26. Bonnie Campbell (ed.), *Regulating Mining in Africa. For whose benefit?* 2004. 89 pp. ISBN 91-7106-527-X

27. Suzanne Dansereau and Mario Zamponi, *Zimbabwe – The Political Economy of Decline.* Compiled by Henning Melber. 2005. 43 pp. ISBN 91-7106-541-5

28. Lars Buur and Helene Maria Kyed, *State Recognition of Traditional Authority in Mozambique. The Nexus of Community Representation and State Assistance.* 2005. 30 pp. ISBN 91-7106-547-4

29. Hans Eriksson and Björn Hagströmer, *Chad – Towards Democratisation or Petro-Dictatorship?* 2005. 82 pp. ISBN 91-7106-549-0

30. Mai Palmberg and Ranka Primorac (eds), *Skinning the Skunk – Facing Zimbabwean Futures.* 2005. 40 pp. ISBN 91-7106-552-0

31. Michael Brüntrup, Henning Melber and Ian Taylor, *Africa, Regional Cooperation and the World Market – Socio-Economic Strategies in Times of Global Trade Regimes.* Compiled by Henning Melber. 2006. 70 pp. ISBN 91-7106-559-8

32. Fibian Kavulani Lukalo, *Extended Handshake or Wrestling Match? – Youth and Urban Culture Celebrating Politics in Kenya.* 2006. 58 pp. ISBN 91-7106-567-9

33. Tekeste Negash, *Education in Ethiopia: From Crisis to the Brink of Collapse.* 2006. 55 pp. ISBN 91-7106-576-8

34. Fredrik Söderbaum and Ian Taylor (eds), *Micro-Regionalism in West Africa. Evidence from Two Case Studies.* 2006. 32 pp. ISBN 91-7106-584-9

35. Henning Melber (ed.), *On Africa – Scholars and African Studies.* 2006. 68 pp. ISBN 978-91-7106-585-8

36. Amadu Sesay, *Does One Size Fit All? The Sierra Leone Truth and Reconciliation Commission Revisited.* 2007. 56 pp. ISBN 978-91-7106-586-5

37. Karolina Hulterström, Amin Y. Kamete and Henning Melber, *Political Opposition in African Countries – The Case of Kenya, Namibia, Zambia and Zimbabwe.* 2007. 86 pp. ISBN 978-7106-587-2

38. Henning Melber (ed.), *Governance and State Delivery in Southern Africa. Examples from Botswana, Namibia and Zimbabwe.* 2007. 65 pp. ISBN 978-91-7106-587-2

39. Cyril Obi (ed.), *Perspectives on Côte d'Ivoire: Between Political Breakdown and Post-Conflict Peace.* 2007. 66 pp. ISBN 978-91-7106-606-6

40. Anna Chitando, *Imagining a Peaceful Society. A Vision of Children's Literature in a Post-Conflict Zimbabwe.* 2008. 26 pp. ISBN 978-91-7106-623-7

41. Olawale Ismail, *The Dynamics of Post-Conflict Reconstruction and Peace Building in West Africa. Between Change and Stability.* 2009. 52 pp. ISBN 978-91-7106-637-4

42. Ron Sandrey and Hannah Edinger, *Examining the South Africa–China Agricultural Trading Relationship.* 2009. 58 pp. ISBN 978-91-7106-643-5

43. Xuan Gao, *The Proliferation of Anti-Dumping and Poor Governance in Emerging Economies.* 2009. 41 pp. ISBN 978-91-7106-644-2

44. Lawal Mohammed Marafa, *Africa's Business and Development Relationship with China. Seeking Moral and Capital Values of the Last Economic Frontier.* 2009. 21 pp. ISBN 978-91-7106-645-9

45. Mwangi wa Githinji, *Is That a Dragon or an Elephant on Your Ladder? The Potential Impact of China and India on Export Led Growth in African Countries.* 2009. 40 pp. ISBN 978-91-7106-646-6

46. Jo-Ansie van Wyk, *Cadres, Capitalists, Elites and Coalitions. The ANC, Business and Development in South Africa.* 2009. 61 pp. ISBN 978-91-7106-656-5

47. Elias Courson, *Movement for the Emancipation of the Niger Delta (MEND). Political Marginalization, Repression and Petro-Insurgency in the Niger Delta.* 2009. 30 pp. ISBN 978-91-7106-657-2

48. Babatunde Ahonsi, *Gender Violence and HIV/AIDS in Post-Conflict West Africa. Issues and Responses.* 2010. 38 pp. ISBN 978-91-7106-665-7

49. Usman Tar and Abba Gana Shettima,
    Endangered Democracy? The Struggle over
    Secularism and its Implications for Politics
    and Democracy in Nigeria.
    2010. 21 pp. ISBN 978-91-7106-666-4

50. Garth Andrew Myers, *Seven Themes in*
    African Urban Dynamics.
    2010. 28 pp. ISBN 978-91-7106-677-0

51. Abdoumaliq Simone, *The Social Infra-*
    structures of City Life in Contemporary
    Africa.
    2010. 33 pp. ISBN 978-91-7106-678-7

52. Li Anshan, *Chinese Medical Cooperation*
    in Africa. With Special Emphasis
    on the Medical Teams and Anti-Malaria
    Campaign.
    2011. 24 pp. ISBN 978-91-7106-683-1

53. Folashade Hunsu, *Zangbeto*: *Navigating the*
    Spaces Between Oral art, Communal Security
    And Conflict Mediation in Badagry, Nigeria.
    2011. 27 pp. ISBN 978-91-7106-688-6

54. Jeremiah O. Arowosegbe, *Reflections on the*
    Challenge of Reconstructing Post-Conflict
    States in West Africa, Insights From Claude
    Ake's Political Writings.
    2011. 40 pp. ISBN 978-91-7106-689-3

www.ingramcontent.com/pod-product-compliance
Lightning Source LLC
Chambersburg PA
CBHW080210300326
41934CB00039B/3437